T0246282

WILDLIFE

Wild-
life

Wildlife

Whether it's looking out of the window into our own backyard or exploring in the wilderness, an encounter with a wild animal – from a tiny squirrel to a mighty lion – can bring joy and wonder and brighten anyone's day.

Immersing yourself in wildlife and nature is good for the soul and for mental health, and has inspired many a writer and commentator over the years. This book combines stunning artworks of animals big and small with quotes about them – some from famous people and others less well-known.

Let us take you on a journey to rainforests, icy wastes and African savannas, exploring the world's wild creatures and what they can teach us about life.

"I meant what I said
and I said what I meant.
An elephant's faithful
one hundred per cent!"

– DR SEUSS

"There is lace in every living thing: the bare branches of winter, the patterns of clouds, the surface of water as it ripples in the breeze... Even a wild dog's matted fur shows a lacy pattern if you look at it closely enough."

– BRUNONIA BARRY

"When you are in a pit of vipers, you have only one choice, bite first."

– REHAN KHAN

"*I couldn't be more chuffed if I were a badger at the start of the mating season!*"

– IAN HOLLOWAY

"*I am about to take my last voyage, a great leap in the dark.*"

– THOMAS HOBBES

"The best way of being kind
to bears is not to be very close
to them."

– MARGARET ATWOOD

"Chimpanzees, gorillas and orangutans have been living for hundreds of thousands of years in their forest, living fantastic lives, never overpopulating, never destroying the forest. I would say that they have been in a way more successful than us as far as being in harmony with the environment."

– JANE GOODALL

"To me, *fast food is when a cheetah eats an antelope.*"

– GEORGE CARLIN

"Sharks are beautiful animals, and if you're lucky enough to see lots of them, that means that you're in a healthy ocean. You should be afraid if you are in the ocean and don't see sharks."

– SYLVIA EARLE

"*If the book is good, is about something that you know, and is truly written, and reading it over you see that this is so, you can let the boys yip and the noise will have that pleasant sound coyotes make on a very cold night when they are out in the snow and you are in your own cabin that you have built or paid for with your work.*"

– ERNEST HEMINGWAY

"In real life, of course, it is the hare that wins. Every time. Look around you."

– ANITA BROOKNER

"I am now a turtle. Virtually everything I own is on my back and suffice it to say I am one ton lighter and therefore 2,000 pounds happier. All houses are gone."

– BOBBY DARIN

"*If we cannot sing of faith and triumph, we will sing our despair. We will be that kind of bird. There are day owls, and there are night owls, and each is beautiful and even musical while about its business.*"

– HENRY DAVID THOREAU

"My heart's in the Highlands, my heart is not here;
My heart's in the Highlands a-chasing the deer."

– ROBERT BURNS

"*It seems to me that the natural world is the greatest source of excitement; the greatest source of visual beauty; the greatest source of intellectual interest. It is the greatest source of so much in life that makes life worth living.*"

– DAVID ATTENBOROUGH

"Well as giraffes say, 'you don't get no leaves unless you stick your neck out'."

– SID WADDELL

"*The leech's kiss, the squid's embrace, The prurient ape's defiling touch: And do you like the human race?*
No, not much."

– ALDOUS HUXLEY

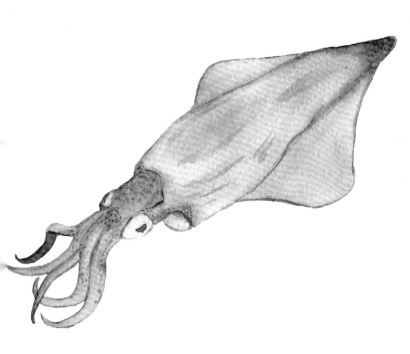

"A flock of flirting flamingos
is pure, passionate,
pink pandemonium –
a frenetic flamingle-mangle
– a discordant discotheque
of delirious dancing,
flamboyant feathers,
and flamingo lingo."

– CHARLEY HARPER

"Cultures have long heard wisdom in non-human voices: Apollo, god of music, medicine and knowledge, came to Delphi in the form of a dolphin. But dolphins, which fill the oceans with blipping and chirping, and whales, which mew and caw in ultramarine jazz – a true rhapsody in blue – are hunted to the edge of silence."

– JAY GRIFFITHS

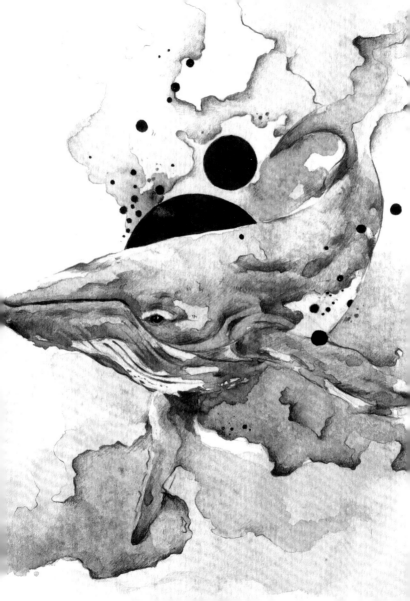

"On my mother's side
I'm Polish-Jewish, and
on my father's side
I'm Scottish puffin."

– TAMSIN GREIG

"*I have been honoured to serve the whales, dolphins, seals – and all the other creatures on this Earth. Their beauty, intelligence, strength, and spirit have inspired me.*"

– PAUL WATSON

*"If wits were pins,
the man would be a
veritable hedgehog."*

– FRANCES HARDINGE

"*I feel more comfortable with gorillas than people. I can anticipate what a gorilla is going to do, and they're purely motivated.*"

– DIAN FOSSEY

"*I have a lot of chameleon qualities, I get very absorbed in my surroundings.*"

– RIVER PHOENIX

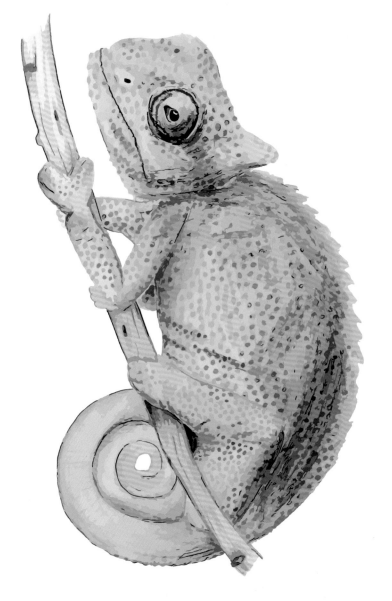

"Those who awaken never rest in one place. Like swans, they rise and leave the lake. On the air they rise and fly an invisible course. Their food is knowledge. They live on emptiness. They have seen how to break free. Who can follow them?"

– BUDDHA

"She's so dark, so harsh, so wounded. Her prickly exterior would keep most everyone away.
And yet all I want to do is get closer."

– K A TUCKER

"I remember when I was younger, and in school, our teachers showed us films of plastic in the ocean, starving Polar Bears and so on. I cried through all the movies. My classmates were concerned when they watched the film, but when it stopped, they started thinking about other things. I couldn't do that. Those pictures were stuck in my head."

– GRETA THUNBERG

"*It is possible to fly without motors, but not without knowledge and skill.*"

– WILBUR WRIGHT

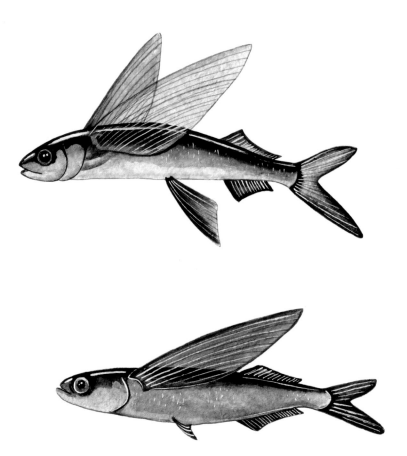

"Life began with waking up and loving my mother's face."

– GEORGE ELIOT

"National Geographic contacted me about getting on their label, and I was like, 'Wow, I want to be label mates with the sharks and lemurs'."

– BJÖRK

"On motionless wing they emerge from the lifting mists, sweep a final arc of sky, and settle in clangorous descending spirals to their feeding grounds. A new day has begun on the crane marsh."

– ALDO LEOPOLD

"When you come across a problem in your life, do not always try to solve it; make a long jump like a kangaroo and continue on your way! Sometimes problems must be leapt over without touching them"

– MEHMET MURAT ILDAN

"*I'm not a diva.*
I'm a tadpole
trying to be a frog."

– TONI BRAXTON

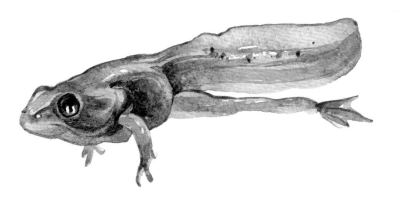

"A fox should not be on the jury at a goose's trial."

– THOMAS FULLER

"Dogs, monkeys, and parrots are a thousand times less miserable than we are."

– VOLTAIRE

"*I have no fear of losing my life – if I have to save a koala or a crocodile or a kangaroo or a snake, mate, I will save it.*"

– STEVE IRWIN

"A squirrel is just a rat
with a cuter outfit!"

– SARAH JESSICA PARKER

"Is a Hippopotamus a Hippopotamus, or just a really cool Opotamus?"

– MITCH HEDBERG

"*I did find out about the koalas and how eucalyptus makes them high and why they sleep all day. They're little druggies.*"

– KRISTEN BELL

"*The python dropped his head lightly for a moment on Mowgli's shoulders. 'A brave heart and a courteous tongue,' said he. 'They shall carry thee far through the jungle, manling. But now go hence quickly with thy friends. Go and sleep, for the moon sets and what follows it is not well that thou shouldst see'.*"

– RUDYARD KIPLING

*"If I had to choose,
I would rather have birds
than airplanes."*

– CHARLES LINDBERGH

"A world without huge regions of total wilderness would be a cage; a world without lions and tigers and vultures and snakes and elk and bison would be – will be – a human zoo. A high-tech slum."

– EDWARD ABBEY

"Some days I think I look kind of cute, but other days I try to avoid the mirror."

– DAVID ALAN GRIER

"My parents used to call me 'The Little Frog,' because whenever they asked how I knew something, I'd say 'read it,' which sounds a bit like a frog croak."

– TALULAH RILEY

"*Every time Europe looks across the Atlantic to see the American Eagle, it observes only the rear end of an ostrich.*"

– H G WELLS

"'The time has come,'
the walrus said,
'to talk of many things:
of shoes and ships
– and sealing wax –
of cabbages and kings.'"

– LEWIS CARROLL

"Great people will always
be mocked by those who feel
smaller than them. A lion
does not flinch at laughter
coming from a hyena."

– SUZY KASSEM

"It was a mating dance only slightly more dignified than presenting like a mandrill, but endearing in its own fashion."

– JAMES S A COREY

"*I always liked red.
It's a picker-upper.*"

– NANCY REAGAN

"*Knowledge is like a lion;*
it cannot be gently embraced."

– SOUTH AFRICAN PROVERB

"But now that I know it's possible for a couple of zebras to outsmart a crocodile, life is starting to look up."

– SARAH WEEKS

"Somebody said that writers are like otters. Otters, if they do a trick and you give them a fish, the next time they'll do a better trick or a different trick because they'd already done that one. And writers tend to be otters. Most of us get pretty bored doing the same trick. We've done it, so let's do something different."

– NEIL GAIMAN

"People can have rhinoceros skin, but there's a point when something's going to hurt you."

– JANET JACKSON

"*The autumn always gets me badly, as it breaks into colours. I want to go south, where there is no autumn, where the cold doesn't crouch over one like a Snow Leopard waiting to pounce.*"

– D H LAWRENCE

"*That was pretty easy, and I wrote it while delousing my pet tapir.*"

– GREG GUTFELD

"Water was how the desert would bring everyone together. The antelope's daily prayer, weighing the mortal need of water with the mortal danger of obtaining it."

– MIKE BOND

"*He looked like a vulture dissatisfied with its breakfast corpse.*"

– P G WODEHOUSE

"A lorry-load of tortoises crashed into a train-load of terrapins. I thought: 'That's a turtle disaster'."

– TOMMY COOPER

"I know animals more gallant than the African warthog, but none more courageous. He is the peasant of the plains – the drab and dowdy digger in the earth. He is the uncomely but intrepid defender of family, home, and bourgeois convention, and he will fight anything of any size that intrudes upon his smug existence."

– BERYL MARKHAM

"*I'm a big believer in digging deep when I travel to a new place.*"

– MELISSA LEONG

"Wolves don't lose sleep over the opinion of sheep."

– ARISTOTLE

Published in 2023 by Reed New Holland Publishers
Sydney

Level 1, 178 Fox Valley Road, Wahroonga, NSW 2076, Australia

newhollandpublishers.com

A record of this book is held at the National Library of Australia.

ISBN 978 1 92107 355 7

Managing Director: Fiona Schultz
Publisher and Project Editor: Simon Papps
Designer: Andrew Davies
Production Director: Arlene Gippert
Printed in China

10 9 8 7 6 5 4 3 2 1

OTHER TITLES BY REED NEW HOLLAND INCLUDE:

A Complete Guide to Reptiles of Australia. Sixth Edition
Steve Wilson and Gerry Swan
ISBN 978 1 92554 671 2

The Slater Field Guide to Australian Birds. Second Edition
Peter Slater, Pat Slater and Raoul Slater
ISBN 978 1 87706 963 5

Chris Humfrey's Awesome Australian Animals
Chris Humfrey
ISBN 978 1 92554 670 5

Australian Wildlife On Your Doorstep. Second Edition
Stephanie Jackson
ISBN 978 1 92107 320 5

A First Book of Beautiful Bird Songs (book with speaker)
Fred van Gessel
ISBN 978 1 92554 677 4

A First Book of Australian Backyard Wildlife Sounds (book with speaker)
Fred van Gessel
ISBN 978 1 92554 685 9

For details of these books and hundreds of other Natural History titles see

newhollandpublishers.com and follow ReedNewHolland on Facebook